D1030712

HEALTHY OCEANS

Why They Matter

Andrea C. Nakaya

ReferencePoint Press®

San Diego, CA

About the Author

Andrea C. Nakaya, a native of New Zealand, holds a BA in English and an MA in communications from San Diego State University. She has written and edited numerous articles and more than fifty books on current issues. She currently lives in Eagle, Idaho, with her husband and their two children, Natalie and Shane.

© 2023 ReferencePoint Press, Inc.
Printed in the United States

For more information, contact:
ReferencePoint Press, Inc.
PO Box 27779
San Diego, CA 92198
www.ReferencePointPress.com

Picture Credits:
Cover: Sergey Lisitsyn/iStock

6: Vlad61/Shutterstock
10: BlueRingMedia/Shutterstock
12: Choksawatdikorn/Shutterstock
16: Art Wager/iStock
20: imageBROKER/Alamy Stock Photo
23: Ethan Daniels/Shutterstock
26: ULora/iStock

30: IgnacioFPV/Shutterstock
32: Kev Gregory/Shutterstock
35: Reuters/Alamy Stock Photo
38: Bluesky31/Shutterstock
43: Paulo de Oliveira/NHPA/Avalon/Newscom
44: Andrew B Hall/Shutterstock
47: LukaKikina/Shutterstock
51: Tada Images/Shutterstock
54: Jason Escalona/Shutterstock

LIBRARY OF CONGRESS CATALOGING-IN-PUBLICATION DATA

Names: Nakaya, Andrea C., 1976- author.
Title: Healthy oceans : why they matter / by Andrea C. Nakaya.
Description: San Diego, CA : ReferencePoint Press, Inc., 2023. | Includes
   bibliographical references and index.
Identifiers: LCCN 2021058180 (print) | LCCN 2021058181 (ebook) | ISBN
   9781678203405 (Library Binding) | ISBN 9781678203412 (eBook)
Subjects: LCSH: Marine resources conservation--Juvenile literature. |
   Marine pollution--Juvenile literature. | Marine ecology--Juvenile
   literature. | Oceanography--Juvenile literature.
Classification: LCC GC1018 .N35 2023 (print) | LCC GC1018 (ebook) | DDC
   577.7/27--dc23/eng 20220314
LC record available at https://lccn.loc.gov/2021058180
LC ebook record available at https://lccn.loc.gov/2021058181

CONTENTS

More Important than Most People Realize

The health of the oceans is something a lot of people worry about. In 2020 and 2021, the Nippon Foundation (a global philanthropic organization) surveyed thousands of people around the world and found that 83 percent of them felt concerned about issues affecting the oceans. About a quarter said they were very concerned. When asked who should take responsibility for the health of the oceans, many of those surveyed agreed that the actions of business and governments are important, and almost three-quarters said that regular citizens also play a significant role. These findings are not unusual. In survey after survey, researchers have found that most people are worried about the oceans and believe that more needs to be done to keep them healthy.

Deteriorating Health

Despite the high level of concern, every year the health of the world's oceans worsens. In a 2020 examination of ocean pollution published in the *Annals of Global Health*, the authors detail some of the many ways that ocean health is deteriorating. They state:

Climate change and other environmental disruptions of human origin have caused sea surface temperatures to rise, glaciers to melt, and harmful algal species and pathogenic bacteria to migrate into waters that were previously uncontaminated. Rising seas and increasingly violent coastal storms endanger the 600 million people worldwide who live within 10 [meters] of sea level. Rising concentrations of atmospheric [carbon dioxide] have caused acidification of the oceans, which in turn destroys coral reefs, impairs development of oysters and other shellfish, and dissolves calcium-containing microorganisms at the base of the food web. The oceans are losing oxygen. Fish stocks are declining. Dredging, mechanized trawling, oil exploration, and planned deep undersea metal mining threaten the seabeds.[1]

As this long list shows, the reality is that while most people care about the health of the oceans, not enough is being done to protect those oceans. Instead, human activity is causing them to become less and less healthy every year.

This problem is a lot more serious than many people realize. While almost everyone knows that the oceans are important, many do not understand exactly how important they are. The oceans are not just a place to get fish to eat or to enjoy swimming, boating, or surfing. The air that people breathe, the water they drink, and the climate they live in are all bound to the oceans. Humans literally cannot live without oceans. As Karen Sack, president of ocean conservation organization Ocean Unite, stresses, "A healthy ocean is a prerequisite for a healthy planet and healthy human communities."[2] Unfortunately, she warns, as humans inflict more and more damage on the oceans, the oceans are becoming less healthy and less likely to be able to support healthy human communities in the future.

> "A healthy ocean is a prerequisite for a healthy planet and healthy human communities."[2]
>
> —Karen Sack, president of the ocean conservation organization Ocean Unite

Tipping Points

Experts warn that the oceans could eventually be harmed so much that life on earth will be dramatically altered. Thus far, despite pollution and the many other human activities that threaten the oceans, they have proved to be remarkably resilient. The world's oceans continue to support a vast array of living things. However, scientists talk about "tipping points," at which ocean damage could become so great that it cannot be ignored or undone. It is at that point that a cascade of negative effects could forever change life on earth. For instance, some researchers worry that rising ocean temperatures will reach a tipping point, leading to irreversible changes in ocean currents. This in turn could alter the earth's climate, making parts of the world uninhabitable. Another possible tipping point is damage to coral reefs as oceans warm and become too acidic. Coral reefs are extremely important

Earth's coral reefs, like this one in the Red Sea, are home to many different creatures. If unhealthy oceans damage reefs, ocean species that depend on this ecosystem could die out.

to many different creatures. As coral reefs die, many species would probably disappear. This would present a harmful disruption to an ecosystem that provides food for many living creatures, including humans. Owen Gaffney is a global sustainability analyst for the Stockholm Resilience Centre at Stockholm University in Sweden. He warns that the world needs to take the threat of tipping points seriously, saying, "Without emergency action our children are likely to inherit a dangerously destabilised planet."[3]

Experts warn that in order to prevent such a future, society must stop damaging its oceans and make a major effort to repair the damage that has already been done. Further, they argue, this must be done soon, or it might be too late. Volkan Bozkir, president of the United Nations General Assembly, recently spoke about the importance of taking action. His comments echo those of many other advocates for the oceans. He—and they—insist that concern is not enough and that greater action is needed. He says, "Simply speaking, our relationship with our planet's ocean must change." As Bozkir stresses, the oceans are critical to life on earth, and there is "simply no scenario"[4] where humanity could live without them.

> "Simply speaking, our relationship with our planet's ocean must change."[4]
>
> —Volkan Bozkir, president of the United Nations General Assembly

CHAPTER ONE

The Importance of the Oceans

The United States is a huge country, the fourth largest in the world. It is roughly 3,000 miles (4,828 km) wide, and driving from one side to the other takes about six full days. However, the United States is tiny compared to the oceans. In fact, all of the world's countries are small compared to its oceans. All countries put together would cover less than a third of the planet's surface. As the United Nations Environment Programme says, "We live on a blue planet."[5] The bulk of the planet—approximately 70 percent—is not land but blue oceans. It is hard to overstate the importance of these oceans. They cover most of the earth, contain the majority of its living things, and play a critical role in climate and life cycles.

> "We live on a blue planet."[5]
>
> —United Nations Environment Programme, which works to encourage people around the world to care for the environment

Ocean Basics

According to scientists, the world technically has just one global ocean. However, this ocean has been divided into a number of distinct regions, each with its own name. Historically, experts have recognized four of these ocean regions: the Atlantic Ocean, the Pacific Ocean, the Indian Ocean, and the Arctic

Ocean. Most scientific bodies also now recognize a fifth ocean, which has been named the Southern Ocean. It is estimated that all five oceans contain 97 percent of the world's water. Overall, the United Nations estimates that by volume, the oceans make up 99 percent of the earth's living space.

There is enormous variation in what lies at the bottom of these oceans. Just as the surface of the land has valleys, mountains, and plateaus, so does the ocean floor. The National Geographic Society explains some of the features that can be found. It says:

> The ocean contains towering mountain ranges and deep canyons, known as trenches, just like those on land. The peak of the world's tallest mountain—Mount Everest in the Himalaya, measuring 8.84 kilometers (5.49 miles) high—would not even break the surface of the water if it was placed in the Pacific Ocean's Mariana Trench or Philippine Trench, two of the deepest parts of the ocean. On the other hand, the Atlantic Ocean is relatively shallow because large parts of its seafloor are made up of continental shelves—parts of the continents that extend far out into the ocean.[6]

While some of them are deep and some more shallow, overall, the National Geographic Society reports that the average depth of the oceans is about 12,200 feet (3,719 m).

Creatures of the Oceans

The oceans are home to a vast number of different living organisms, the majority of them still unknown to humans. Scientists report that more than 226,000 different ocean species have been

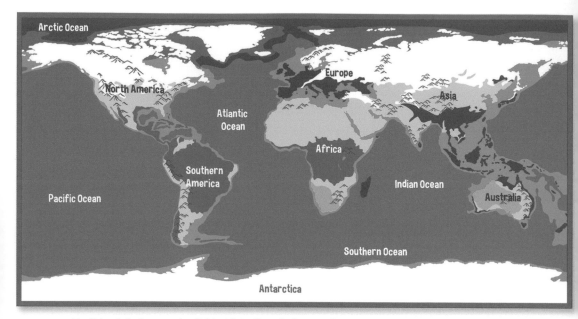

Earth's global ocean is divided into five distinct regions, each with its own name and characteristics. These oceans make up about 99 percent of the earth's living space.

identified so far. However, they recognize that this is just a small percentage of the overall total. The National Oceanic and Atmospheric Administration (NOAA) estimates that 91 percent of ocean species have still not been discovered and classified by scientists, but previously unknown creatures are continually being found. The United Nations Educational, Scientific and Cultural Organization talks about some of the new creatures that have recently been found. It says that large species such as fish, crabs, and marine reptiles continue to be discovered. Overall though, it reports that most new discoveries are smaller types of macroinvertebrates, which are small creatures without a backbone: "The unknown species are composed disproportionately of groups of macroinvertebrates, with tens of thousands of species of smaller crustaceans, molluscs (snails) worms and sponges awaiting discovery."[7] In addition to all the new species that have officially been recognized, the organization adds, tens of thousands of other species have been collected from the oceans by scientists but have not yet been studied or named. Because they have so many different species of living things in them, the oceans are considered to have great biological diversity.

Some of the living things in the oceans will never be discovered by scientists though, because some of those that live there now will not be there in the future. Experts believe that the number of species in the ocean is decreasing every year due to human activities that are harming these organisms and the oceans. For instance, the Caribbean monk seal, the Steller's sea cow, and the sea mink—marine mammals that were all once plentiful—are all thought to be extinct. According to a 2019 report by the Intergovernmental Science-Policy Platform on Biodiversity and Ecosystem Services, more than 33 percent of marine mammals are facing the threat of extinction, and almost 33 percent of sharks and related species are equally threatened.

Phytoplankton and Oxygen

Of all the living things in the oceans, one of the most important is one of the smallest. Phytoplankton are microscopic organisms that drift around in the water, carried by tides and currents. While they are too tiny to be seen without a microscope, phytoplankton are critical to the health of the oceans. This is because the entire ocean food chain starts with these creatures. Phytoplankton are eaten by small ocean creatures, which are then eaten by larger ocean creatures, and so on, up the food chain. Without phytoplankton, both small and large creatures in the ocean would have nothing to eat.

Phytoplankton also do something else critical to life in the oceans and on land: they produce oxygen. Just like land-based plants, they do this through photosynthesis. During photosynthesis, phytoplankton use energy from the sun to produce their own energy. In the process, phytoplankton also absorb carbon dioxide and produce oxygen—a lot of oxygen. For instance, says NOAA's National Ocean Service, "One particular species, Prochlorococcus, is the smallest photosynthetic organism on Earth. But this little bacteria produces up to 20% of the oxygen in our entire

Microscopic phytoplankton drift throughout the world's oceans. As the base of the oceanic food chain, they are essential to the health and nutrition of every ocean animal.

biosphere. That's a higher percentage than all of the tropical rain-forests on land combined."[8] NOAA estimates that the oceans produce at least half of—and up to 80 percent of—the earth's oxygen. While some of this oxygen is used by creatures on land, much of it is actually used by the creatures that live in the oceans.

Weather and Climate

In addition to producing oxygen, the oceans regulate climate and weather. They do this in a number of different ways. One is through the water cycle. The earth's water is always moving, in a process known as the water cycle. At its simplest, the water cycle is an endless loop in which water evaporates from the surface of the oceans, rivers, and lakes—or the land—and goes up into the atmosphere. It then cools down and condenses into rain or snow and falls back onto the land or into bodies of water. This water eventually evaporates into the atmosphere again, and it continues through the same cycle forever. Because the oceans hold most of the earth's water and cover most of the earth's surface, they play a critical part in this water cycle. Most of the rain or snow that falls on the land actually comes from the oceans.

The oceans also affect climate by absorbing heat from the sun and moving that heat around the world through ocean currents. The earth gets a lot of heat from the sun, and the oceans absorb most of that. Without the oceans to absorb the sun's heat, the earth would be much hotter. The heat that goes into the oceans does not just stay in one place, however. Instead, ocean water is constantly moving, and with it, so is the sun's heat. Sean Fleming, senior writer for the World Economic Forum, explains that this heat "tends to be at its most intense nearer the equator, with the water nearest the surface warming the most. Sea currents then transport that heat around the world; north and south, towards the poles."[9]

Unexplored Ocean Depths

Most of the earth's land areas have now been explored by humans; however, that is not the case with the planet's oceans. Although scientists know what some parts of the ocean floor look like, there is a lot about the oceans that remains unknown. Scientists are constantly working to learn more, but because the oceans are so vast and so deep, they are difficult to explore. According to NOAA, even with modern technology, only about 10 percent of the ocean floor has been mapped. Most of the seabed remains unexplored. The National Geographic Society comments, "A far greater percentage of the surfaces of the moon and the planet Mars has been mapped and studied than of our own ocean floor."

National Geographic Society, "Ocean," 2021. www.nationalgeographic.org.

Without ocean currents, many climates would be quite different. NOAA explains, "Regional temperatures would be more extreme—super hot at the equator and frigid toward the poles—and much less of Earth's land would be habitable."[10] Fleming gives an example of how climate would change dramatically without the existing system of currents. He says, "One example is the Gulf Stream, which takes warmer water from the Gulf of Mexico across the Atlantic to Europe. If the Gulf Stream were disrupted, much of the western part of Europe—including the UK, Ireland and France—could become colder."[11]

In the process of moving heat and water, the oceans also drive weather systems. For instance, ocean water is always evaporating into the atmosphere, where it forms rain clouds. These clouds are carried to many different places by winds, and the water eventually falls down to the ground as rain. Tropical storms or hurricanes are also connected to the oceans. These storms form by taking large amounts of heat out of the oceans.

A Source of Food and Medicines

Yet another thing that makes the oceans important to people is the fact they are a vital source of food. The World Economic Forum estimates that fish makes up nearly 16 percent of all the animal protein that is eaten daily around the world. In some places—such as many island nations—that percentage is much higher. In addition to fish, the organization says, people eat many different kinds of algae and sea plants. Tadi, a fisher in Indonesia, cannot imagine life without the oceans. Fishing is his way of life. Without fishing, he says, "how would I feed my family?"[12] He takes his canoe out into the ocean every day, searching for something to eat. Anything he catches that he and his family do not eat is sold for money that they use to buy boat fuel, rice, vegetables, and other necessities. In this way, he and the other people who live in his small village depend on the ocean for almost everything.

The oceans do not just provide food. They also serve as a source of medicine. Many antibiotics and other drugs are based

Layers of the Ocean

Scientists classify the water in the oceans into a number of different zones according to depth. The surface layer, called the epipelagic zone, goes down to 650 feet (198 m). Phytoplankton and other creatures such as dolphins, sharks, and some fish live in this zone. From 650 to 3,300 feet (198 to 1006 m) is the mesopelagic zone. Although this zone does not have much light, it is full of life. An article from the Smithsonian Institution's online Ocean Portal explains, "Squid, krill, jellies, and fish are super abundant in this zone. About 90 percent of the world's fish (by weight) live in the mesopelagic—about 10 billion tons of fish." After the mesopelagic zone comes the bathypelagic zone at 3,300 to 13,100 feet (198 to 3,993 m), then the abyssopelagic zone at 13,100 to 19,700 feet (3,993 to 6,005 m), and in some parts of the ocean, the hadalpelagic zone, which is deeper than 19,700 feet (6,005 m). There is no light in these lower levels, so creatures that live there have evolved to be able to live in such conditions. For example, some creatures that live in the deep ocean create their own light in order to attract mates or lure prey.

Danielle Hall, "The Deep Sea," Smithsonian Institution Ocean Portal, 2018. https://ocean.si.edu.

on natural substances. While some of them come from the land, others were discovered in the oceans. Numerous medicines—including drugs that treat pain, inflammation, and cancer—have been developed from organisms that live in the oceans. In light of the fact that only a fraction of the oceans has actually been explored, researchers think it is very likely that there are many valuable medicines still waiting to be discovered there.

Importance for the Economy and for Recreation

Not only do the oceans provide for basic human needs such as food, oxygen, and a stable climate, they are also vital to the

Massive cargo container ships ply the waters of the world's oceans. The shipping industry employs over 1 million people worldwide.

economy. A lot of people earn a living by doing something that is connected to the oceans. NOAA reports that in the United States, one in every six jobs is related to the oceans and that the oceans support more than 28 million jobs overall. Ocean-related jobs include work in the fishing and boating industry, ocean transport, and tourism and recreation. Fishing is one of the most important ocean-related jobs, and the World Wildlife Fund reports that worldwide, more than 200 million people rely on fishing as their main source of income.

The oceans are also an important part of recreation. Ocean recreation includes swimming, surfing, sportfishing, diving, and boating. The Ocean Foundation says that every year, more than 180 million people go to US beaches for recreation. Many people feel a strong attraction to the oceans. Marine biologist Wallace J. Nichols wrote a book called *Blue Mind*, about the positive effects that the oceans and other bodies of water have on people. He says, "Research has shown that being near, in, on or under water can provide a long list of benefits for our mind and body, including lowering stress and anxiety, increasing an overall sense of well-being and happiness, a lower heart and breathing rate."[13] In 2021 the Ocean Conservation Trust surveyed thousands of people in the United Kingdom and found that most of them felt a strong connection to the ocean. Eighty percent believed the ocean was good for their physical health, and 84 percent believed it benefited their mental health.

> "Research has shown that being near, in, on or under water can provide a long list of benefits for our mind and body."[13]
>
> —Wallace J. Nichols, a marine biologist

The oceans are vital to life on earth. However, they are a lot more vulnerable than many people realize. The Marine Conservation Institute says, "For far too long, people assumed that the ocean was limitless and immune to human impacts."[14] The realization that this is not the case has been growing. Just as people depend on the oceans for their health and well-being, the oceans depend on people for their health and well-being.

CHAPTER TWO

Climate Change

In the summer of 2021, a record-breaking heat wave struck the Pacific Northwest of the United States and the western coast of Canada. It was so hot that roads buckled and power lines melted. Hundreds of people died. In the oceans, the death toll was much higher. The Ocean Conservancy estimates that as many as 1 billion marine creatures living in the intertidal zone—the area that is underwater at high tide and exposed to the air at low tide—died during the heat wave. The organization says, "Scores of mussels, clams, barnacles, snails and sea stars died struggling to survive the extreme and unrelenting heat, literally cooked alive."[15]

The World Weather Attribution initiative studied the heat wave and concluded that it was strongly related to climate change. The organization says, "An event such as the Pacific Northwest 2021 heatwave is still rare or extremely rare in today's climate, yet would be virtually impossible without human-caused climate change." In the future, predicts the organization, "as warming continues, it will become a lot less rare."[16] Of all the threats faced by the oceans, climate change is one of the greatest. There is evidence that it is substantially changing the oceans and that this will mean significant harmful impacts for the entire world in the future.

How Climate Change Is Altering the Oceans

One of the main ways that climate change is altering the oceans is by heating them up. Most people know that climate change is causing global temperatures to rise. For instance, according to the National Aeronautics and Space Administration (NASA), 2020 and 2016 tie as the hottest years on record since 1880, when record keeping began. The temperature is not just increasing on land, it is also rising in the oceans. In fact, the oceans are absorbing a lot more heat than the land is. According to a 2019 report by the Intergovernmental Panel on Climate Change (IPCC), as global temperatures have increased, more than 90 percent of the extra heat coming into the climate system has been absorbed by the oceans. As a result, the temperature of the oceans has been steadily increasing. In a study published in 2021 in *Advances in Atmospheric Sciences*, researchers presented the results of an analysis of historical ocean temperatures. They found that the oceans are getting warmer every decade and that in 2020 overall ocean temperatures were the hottest ever recorded. Marine heat waves—in which ocean water temperatures become abnormally high in a specific area for a certain period of time—are also becoming increasingly frequent. The IPCC says that marine heat waves have become more intense and have very likely doubled in frequency over the past forty years.

Climate change is also causing the concentration of carbon in the oceans to increase. That carbon is coming from the atmosphere. The earth's atmosphere is made up of a number of different gases, including carbon dioxide. Some carbon dioxide is necessary for living things. For instance, phytoplankton in the oceans and plants on the land use it for photosynthesis. However, since the Industrial Revolution of the eighteenth and nineteenth centuries, humans have been creating more and more carbon dioxide through activities such as burning fossil fuels for transportation and energy. This is causing the amount of carbon dioxide in the atmosphere to increase dramatically. According to NASA, the amount of carbon dioxide in the earth's atmosphere has increased 47 percent since the beginning of the industrial age.

Beluga whales, like this one, thrive in the icy Arctic waters and are one of many species that are being negatively impacted by rising water temperatures and carbon concentrations.

All that extra carbon dioxide—along with other greenhouse gases—is causing world temperatures to get warmer. But the carbon is not all staying in the atmosphere. Carbon dioxide dissolves in water, and scientists have discovered that large amounts of the extra carbon in the atmosphere are actually being absorbed by the oceans. This has benefited people in one way because it has reduced the amount of atmospheric warming. However, the increase in carbon is changing ocean chemistry and making the oceans more acidic. The United Nations reports that ocean acidity has increased 26 percent since the beginning of the Industrial Revolution. Higher acidity has negative effects on many marine plants and animals. For instance, it makes it harder for some creatures such as shellfish and coral to build the protective shells or skeletons that they need to survive.

How Changes Affect Ocean Life

Rising temperatures and carbon concentrations are having negative effects on many of the creatures that live in the oceans. The

IPCC reports that since 1950, a large number of marine creatures have changed their behavior and where they live as a result of ocean warming. It says, "This has resulted in shifts in species composition, abundance and biomass production of ecosystems, from the equator to the poles." While some creatures have become more abundant, for example, many have become much less plentiful. Further, the IPCC explains, changes in some creatures have led to changes in many others. "Altered interactions between species have caused cascading impacts on ecosystem structure and functioning,"[17] it says.

NOAA scientist Nick Bond talks about cascading impacts in the context of marine heat waves, which scientists believe have

Sea Level Rise and the Marshall Islands

Rising oceans threaten people who live in coastal areas. As sea levels rise, they cause erosion and flooding, which can contaminate freshwater in the ground with salt. Ultimately, rising sea levels can lead to the displacement of coastal communities. The Marshall Islands in the Pacific Ocean are already being affected by these problems. Flooding has increased, and freshwater supplies are becoming contaminated by saltwater. Former Marshall Islands president Hilda Heine says that the situation gets worse every year. "Water comes over my own seawall here in my garden every month," she says. "Other global leaders may not take this so seriously, but we can't close our eyes." The nation's leaders have repeatedly expressed frustration with the rest of the world for not taking action to stop climate change. Heine says, "While the world talks about climate change, for us it's an existential threat." She worries about what will happen if the Marshallese are forced to move elsewhere, explaining, "We see our culture and language as very much tied to the land. If we had to pick up and go, there is no guarantee these would survive."

Quoted in Nicola Milne, "'We Can't Close Our Eyes' to Climate Change, Says Marshall Isles Ex-President," Reuters, January 15, 2020. www.reuters.com.

become more common as a result of climate change. He explains that these heat waves affect the growth of zooplankton. Many sea creatures rely on these microscopic creatures for food, so any changes to their population can have significant effects throughout the whole ocean food web. During marine heat waves, Bond states, "the zooplankton are smaller and don't have as much fat in them. For a lot of seabirds, marine mammals and small fish, these zooplankton are just not as good as the ones that are bigger and have more fat and calories."[18] The presence of smaller zooplankton does not just mean that seabirds, marine mammals, and small fish do not get enough food. It also affects the creatures that eat those small fish, and the creatures that eat those creatures, and so on. Overall, if any ocean animals or plants are less healthy, entire ecosystems that interact with them can be less healthy.

Kelp is an example of how all the creatures in an ecosystem are important and how damage to one can be very harmful to the rest. Environmental writer Lucy Sherriff explains the importance of kelp in the ocean ecosystem. She says, "Kelp are essentially the ocean's equivalent of trees. They absorb carbon dioxide and nitrogen compounds, helping clean the atmosphere while capturing up to 20 times more carbon per acre than land forests. They also provide a vital habitat for a broad range of marine life; without them, entire ocean ecosystems would crumble."[19]

Researchers who study the health of kelp forests have identified a troubling trend: the world's kelp forests are disappearing as a result of climate change. This loss could have dire consequences for all the other creatures that depend on these forests. According to the National Science Foundation, kelp forests off the Northern California coast have already declined by 95 percent after ocean warming left the kelp weak and vulnerable to predators. This once-thriving region of sea life has been inundated by sea urchins, which have a voracious appetite for kelp. As kelp forests disappear, so do the many species that once lived there. The National Science Foundation says, "Species-rich kelp forests have been replaced by 'urchin barrens,' where purple sea urchins cover a seafloor devoid of kelp and other algae."[20]

Coral Reefs

Like kelp forests, coral reefs also support many different living creatures, and they are also experiencing great harm due to climate change. First, coral reefs are harmed by the increased acidity in the oceans, which makes it more difficult for them to grow and to repair themselves. Second, they are being harmed by rising water temperatures. Warmer water can slow their growth and can cause disease. It can also lead to a catastrophic event called bleaching. NPR climate change correspondent Lauren Sommer explains, "Corals live in a domestic partnership, of sorts, with microscopic algae. The algae provide food for corals, not to mention their vibrant colors. But under periods of intense heat stress, the corals expel the algae, leaving only white skeletons." This is called bleaching. While some reefs can recover after bleaching, for many it is lethal. In her 2021 report she notes, "These mass bleaching

Healthy coral gets its color from algae. Due to over-warm water conditions, the coral expels the algae and becomes white—an event called bleaching.

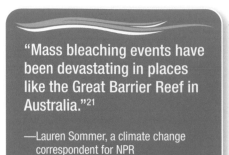
events have been devastating in places like the Great Barrier Reef in Australia, which has experienced three in the last five years."[21]

The world's coral reefs are declining so much that some experts worry that they will soon disappear. United Nations special envoy for the ocean Peter Thomson says, "The UN's Intergovernmental Panel on Climate Change (IPCC) special report on global warming tells us that once global temperatures increase beyond 2°C above pre-industrial levels, we will lose the great majority of the planet's living coral reefs. Meanwhile, the World Meteorological Organization (WMO) warns us that on our current path of carbon dioxide emissions, we are heading towards a temperature increase of 3° to 5°C by the end of this century."[22] He stresses that the loss of coral reefs would be disastrous because they support about 30 percent of the biodiversity in the oceans, so losing them would mean a massive loss of other types of ocean life.

Ocean Currents and Climate

Researchers worry that as the oceans become warmer, they will also alter important systems of currents, and this could have devastating consequences in terms of weather and climate. This is because ocean currents play an important part in regulating the climate, and if they change, climate could change dramatically too. The current system known as the Atlantic Meridional Overturning Circulation (AMOC) provides an example. This current system picks up warm, salty water from the tropics, carries it to northern Europe, and then takes cold water back southward along the floor of the ocean. This redistribution of heat plays an essential part in climate and weather around the world. Some scientists worry that climate change could cause the AMOC to fail and that this could have disas-

The Likelihood of More Destructive Hurricanes

Ocean temperatures have a significant impact on how hurricanes develop. Warm ocean water helps fuel hurricanes. As the oceans continue to warm, researchers believe, hurricanes are likely to form in more places than before and to be stronger than ever. Many researchers insist that hurricanes are already becoming more powerful. "Potential intensity is going up," says Kerry Emanuel, a professor of atmospheric science at the Massachusetts Institute of Technology. "We predicted it would go up 30 years ago, and the observations show it going up." In addition to fueling more powerful hurricanes, climate change has raised the level of the oceans, and this means that when hurricanes do occur, the accompanying storm surges are often more devastating. For instance, "If [Hurricane] Sandy's storm surge had occurred in 1912 rather than 2012," says Emanuel, "It probably wouldn't have flooded Lower Manhattan."

Quoted in Veronica Penney, "What We Know About Climate Change and Hurricanes," *New York Times*, August 29, 2021. www.nytimes.com.

trous consequences. Journalist Sarah Kaplan explains, "Higher temperatures make ocean waters warmer and lighter. An influx of freshwater from melting ice sheets and glaciers dilutes North Atlantic's saltiness, reducing its density. If these waters aren't heavy enough to sink, the entire AMOC will shut down." According to Kaplan, this has already happened in the past. She says, "Studies suggest that toward the end of the last ice age, a massive glacial lake burst through a declining North American ice sheet. The flood of freshwater spilled into the Atlantic, halting the AMOC and plunging much of the Northern Hemisphere—especially Europe—into deep cold."[23] After analyzing gas bubbles that were preserved in polar ice, scientists have estimated that this cold spell was one thousand years long.

Rising Oceans

As climate change causes the oceans to become warmer, it also causes a rise in sea level. Climate change causes this rise in a number of different ways. Sea level rises because the ocean temperature is increasing, and warmer water expands. In addition, climate change is causing the world's ice to melt, and that is adding water to the ocean. While there are variations in different parts of the world, NOAA reports that overall, there was a 4- to 5-inch (10.2 to 12.7 cm) rise in global mean sea level from 1900 to 1990. However, the oceans are rising a lot more rapidly in recent years than ever before. NOAA states that from 1990 to 2015—a span of just twenty-five years—the oceans rose 3 inches (7.6 cm). They are projected to rise anywhere from 1 to 8 feet (30.5 to 244 cm) by 2100.

Coastal communities, like Miami, Florida (pictured), are in danger from a sea level rise of even a few inches.

A few inches of sea level rise might not sound like much. Certainly, it does not sound catastrophic. And yet a 2021 World Bank report warns that as many as 216 million people could become climate migrants by 2050 if society does not take action to reduce

climate change. Climate migrants are people who are forced to move because of rising sea level, decreasing crop productivity, and freshwater shortages—resulting from climate change—that make their communities uninhabitable. Like the rest of the world, the United States is threatened by the rising sea level. According to NOAA, about 40 percent of the US population lives in coastal areas, even though coastal land makes up less than 10 percent of all of the land in the United States. NOAA's National Ocean Service says, "This means that issues that affect the coasts affect a large proportion of Americans."[24]

The US Environmental Protection Agency (EPA) warns that reversing the harms the oceans are experiencing will not be quick or easy, because changes in ocean systems happen over long periods of time. This means that current carbon levels and warming are already causing changes that will continue to happen for a long time in the future. According to the EPA, "Even if greenhouse gas emissions were stabilized tomorrow, it would take many more years—decades to centuries—for the oceans to adjust to changes in the atmosphere and the climate that have already occurred."[25] Even though it is likely to take some time, researchers believe that the condition of the oceans can ultimately be improved by taking action to stop climate change.

CHAPTER THREE

Pollution

Somewhere in the North Pacific Ocean, an area of rotating currents called a gyre pulls marine debris into its center. It is one of five gyres found in the world's oceans. The gyre in the North Pacific is pulling in so much debris that it has been given the nickname "Great Pacific Garbage Patch." Most of the trash the gyre has accumulated comes from land—and most of it is plastic. While there are some standard plastic objects (like bottles and fishing line) trapped in the gyre, most of the plastic is actually in the form of very small pieces. Plastic, it turns out, breaks down quickly in the ocean. As the National Geographic Society notes, "These patches are almost entirely made up of tiny bits of plastic, called microplastics. Microplastics can't always be seen by the naked eye. Even satellite imagery doesn't show a giant patch of garbage. The microplastics of the Great Pacific Garbage Patch can simply make the water look like a cloudy soup. This soup is intermixed with larger items, such as fishing gear and shoes."[26]

Plastic is not the only pollutant in the world's oceans. In one 2020 examination of ocean pollution and human health, researchers concluded, "Pollution of the oceans is widespread, it is worsening, and its geographic extent is expanding. Ocean pollution is a complex and ever-changing mixture of chemicals and biological materials that includes plastic waste, petroleum-based pollutants, toxic metals, manufactured chemicals, pharmaceuticals, pesticides, and a noxious stew of nitrogen, phosphorus, fertilizer, and sewage."[27] The oceans are being greatly harmed by all of these different pollutants.

Plastic

When it comes to pollution in the ocean, plastic is one of the biggest problems. Plastic is cheap to produce and extremely versatile. It is used in packaging, medical devices, cars, clothing, furniture, home appliances, computers, and mobile phones. And when it is no longer needed, it becomes waste. According to the United Nations Environment Programme, every year, the world produces 30 million metric tons of plastic waste. According to a 2021 report by the National Academy of Sciences, the United States produces more plastic waste than any other country. The problem with all that waste is that plastic does not decompose. It breaks down into smaller and smaller pieces, but these pieces stay in the environment. As the world produces more and more plastic every year, more and more plastic is accumulating in the environment. Much of it ends up in the oceans.

Plastic in the oceans comes from many different things. Single-use plastics are a major source of ocean pollution. It is estimated that about half of all the plastic that the world produces consists of single-use items such as water bottles, straws, plastic bags, and food packaging that are used once then thrown away. Another source of plastic in the oceans is discarded fishing gear such as nets, lines, and ropes. Scientist and activist Marcus Eriksen has been on numerous ocean expeditions. He explains, "Nets and buoys are designed to last." Much of this sturdy fishing gear gets lost or discarded, creating new ocean hazards. For example, he says, "lost nets or 'ghost nets' are indiscriminate killers, likely catching more fish when lost than when used for fishing. They become navigational hazards, tangling boat propellers, and wreak ecological havoc, bulldozing coral reefs and tearing coral apart."[28]

Another major source of plastic pollution in the oceans is the clothing

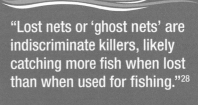

"Lost nets or 'ghost nets' are indiscriminate killers, likely catching more fish when lost than when used for fishing."[28]

—Marcus Eriksen, an activist and scientist

industry. Will McCallum is head of oceans at Greenpeace UK, where he campaigns against plastics. He says, "It comes as a surprise to most people that the clothes they wear are one of the greatest sources of plastic in the ocean. Minuscule strands of clothing, normally made of nylon or polyester and much finer than human hair, are shed from our clothes every time we wear them, wash them, and, of course, when we throw them away."[29]

The oceans are awash in plastic. This, warns the international Environmental Investigation Agency, is a problem of global proportions. "The reach and depth of the contamination is horrifying," the organization states. "Microplastics have been documented in all marine habitats—from the ocean surface and sea ice to the seabed."[30]

How Plastic Harms the Oceans

All that plastic is causing harm in many ways. Scientists have found that it is becoming more and more common for marine creatures to eat plastic. These creatures often do so because they think it is food. For instance, sea turtles eat plastic bags because they mistake them for jellyfish, which are among their favorite foods. Seabirds commonly eat plastic too. On Lord Howe Island, off the eastern coast of Australia, a team of biologists have worked to save shearwater chicks that were dying from plastic. The chicks

Plastic goods, such as bottles and fishing line, break down in the ocean into very small pieces called microplastics. In some areas, these pieces form hundreds of square miles of dangerous debris.

Ocean Animals and Noise Pollution

In addition to polluting the ocean with things like plastic, runoff, and oil, humans are causing another kind of pollution: noise pollution. Oil drilling, military sonar, and shipping all create noise under the water, and that can be disruptive and harmful to the creatures that live there. The National Ocean Service details some of these harms. It says, "Higher noise levels can reduce the ability of animals to communicate with potential mates, other group members, their offspring, or feeding partners. Noise can also reduce an ocean animal's ability to hear environmental cues that are vital for survival, including those key to avoiding predators, finding food, and navigating to preferred habitats." The Ocean Conservancy says that the COVID-19 pandemic has revealed just how much underwater noise is affecting some creatures. It explains:

> When the world came to a halt . . . [in 2020] around COVID-19, international shipping declined 20% in just a few months, resulting in about a 25% decrease in noise in our seas. Due to this decrease, we're seeing in real time how animals can prosper in quieter seas. One study in Alaska found humpback whales socializing, feeding and even napping in once-busy channels. Orcas in Scotland and Canada have been found closer to shore.

National Ocean Service, "What Is Ocean Noise?," February 26, 2021. https://oceanservice.noaa.go.

Ocean Conservancy, "How Does Underwater Noise Impact Our Ocean?," July 7, 2021. https://oceanconservancy.org.

had stomachs so full of plastic that there was no room for food. "It was shocking to see how much would come out of one chick," says Liz Bonnin, who accompanied the group for a BBC documentary about plastics. "We saw, I think 90 pieces come out of one of the chicks on the second night."[31] Even when sea creatures do not directly eat plastic, they often end up eating it when they eat smaller creatures that have done so. For example, a dolphin might be too intelligent to eat a piece of plastic floating in the ocean, but it does eat fish, and many of those fish have eaten microplastics if not larger pieces of plastic.

Eating plastic is harmful in many ways. A stomach full of plastic can cause an animal to starve because it feels full but is not actually getting any nutrition, as in the case of the shearwater chicks. Plastic can also block an animal's digestive system, and sharp pieces can cut its insides. Plastic products also contain toxic chemicals. The Smithsonian Institution's Ocean Portal explains, "Not only does ingesting plastic cause severe physical harm to an animal, it can lead to poisoning as harmful chemicals leach out from the plastic. Flame retardants, antimicrobial agents, and antioxidants (used as a preservative) are common additives to plastics that are known to cause harm to animal health."[32] Further, says the organization, plastic often absorbs other harmful chemicals from the environment, making it even more toxic.

Even if they do not eat it, marine creatures can be harmed just by having plastic in their environment. Many get tangled up in plastic trash and drown. It can also tightly wrap around animals, killing them more slowly by cutting off circulation, cutting into skin as they grow and causing infection, restricting movement, and making it difficult to hunt for food or get away from predators. In

An Atlantic grey seal, caught in the remains of a fishing net, rests on Horsey Beach in Norfolk, England. Without help, this seal will die.

2020 the organization Oceana reported that it had analyzed data from dozens of different agencies that collect information about how plastic affects creatures in the ocean. It says, "Oceana found evidence of nearly 1,800 animals from 40 different species swallowing or becoming entangled in plastic since 2009."[33]

Runoff

Plastic is not the only pollutant that threatens ocean health. Agricultural and industrial runoff is another major source of ocean pollution. The EPA explains how runoff from the land pollutes the oceans:

> As we develop our cities and towns, we replace forests and meadows with buildings and pavement. And now when it rains, the water (often called runoff or stormwater) runs off roofs and driveways into the street. Runoff picks up fertilizer, oil, pesticides, dirt, bacteria and other pollutants as it makes its way through storm drains and ditches—untreated—to our streams, rivers, lakes and the ocean.[34]

The chemicals in this runoff poison both plants and animals that live in the oceans.

Some runoff actually becomes food for certain ocean creatures, but this also ends up harming the oceans. When fertilizer and other agricultural chemicals reach the oceans, they become food for algae. When algae eat large amounts of these chemicals, they grow much more than usual. This is called an algal bloom. The algae grow so dense that they block the sunlight, and marine plants underneath them die. The algae eventually die too. As the dead plants and algae decompose, they reduce the amount of oxygen in the water, which causes other marine life to die off. This process whereby the water becomes

"Runoff picks up fertilizer, oil, pesticides, dirt, bacteria and other pollutants as it makes its way through storm drains and ditches—untreated—to our streams, rivers, lakes and the ocean."[34]

—US Environmental Protection Agency

Pollution and Human Health

Ocean pollution does not just make marine creatures sick. When humans come into contact with polluted water, they can become sick too. One common type of illness that people can get from swimming in polluted ocean water is gastroenteritis, which can cause vomiting, stomachache, diarrhea, and fever. Another common type of pollution-related illness comes from swimming in water with a toxic algal bloom. The toxins from algae can cause skin rashes, vomiting, and diarrhea, and in severe cases they can result in liver or kidney damage. Human illness related to ocean pollution is common. In a 2020 study of ocean pollution and human health, the authors conclude, "Pollution of the oceans poses a clear and present danger to human health. It is causing disease, disability, and premature death in countries around the world today." While anyone can get sick from polluted ocean water, according to the EPA, people with weakened immune systems, the elderly, and children are more susceptible to becoming ill.

Philip J. Landrgian et al., "Human Health and Ocean Pollution," *Annals of Global Health*, December 3, 2020. https://annalsofglobalhealth.org.

excessively enriched with nutrients is known as eutrophication. Some types of algal blooms also cause harm by producing toxins that are dangerous to both animals and humans.

When an area of water has so little oxygen that life cannot survive there, this is known as hypoxia, and the area is often called a dead zone. According to the EPA, the biggest dead zone in the United States is in the Gulf of Mexico—a result of pollution from the Mississippi River. That dead zone, which occurs every summer, is estimated to be more than 6,000 square miles (15,540 sq. km). There are also regular algal blooms off the coast of Florida. In July 2021 the Tampa Bay area experienced an unusually severe bloom that killed large numbers of sea creatures. Journalist Josie Fischels described that algal bloom this way: "Discolored, soupy waters have been lapping the shore, and the beaches are laden with dead, rotting sea life."[35] Area resident Maya Burke also described the scene on the beach: "It's significant numbers of dead fish all up and down the food chain, from small forage fish all the way up to tarpon, manatees, dolphins. . . . If it's swimming in the bay, right now it's washing up dead."[36]

Dead zones are a global phenomenon. Northern Europe's Baltic Sea is believed to have the largest dead zone in the world. In 2019 the European Environment Agency reported that this dead zone had reached a size of more than 23,000 square miles (59,570 sq. km). Overall, the United Nations reports that eutrophication is becoming worse worldwide and warns, "Without concerted efforts, coastal eutrophication is expected to increase in 20 percent of large marine ecosystems by 2050."[37]

Oil Spills

Oil is another source of ocean pollution. Around the world, oil is taken out of the ground or from beneath the ocean floor. It is used to make fuel and a variety of other products, including plastics and paints. Natural seepage takes place in the ocean in small amounts. This is different from spills, which can be small or

A shark swims under an oil slick after a major oil spill off the coast of Huntington Beach, California, in 2021. Oil is poisonous to the plants and animals that live in the ocean.

large. Oil spills are a relatively common occurrence. "Thousands of oil spills occur in U.S. waters each year," NOAA states. "Most of these spills are small, for example when oil spills while refueling a ship. But these spills can still cause damage, especially if they happen in sensitive environments, like beaches, mangroves, and wetlands. Large oil spills are major, dangerous disasters."[38] According to NOAA, large spills are typically the result of a pipeline breaking, an oil tanker sinking, or an oil drilling problem.

In large amounts, oil is not good for the oceans or the living things in them. When oil spills into the oceans, it can coat the creatures that live there and make it difficult for them to survive. For instance, it covers the feathers of birds so that they cannot fly. That is why scientists try to clean the oil off wildlife after a spill. Oil also poisons plants and animals, causing health problems or even death. An oil spill is extremely difficult to clean up, and the harmful effects of oil can be dramatic and long lasting. In 2021 a damaged oil pipeline about 5 miles (8 km) off the coast of Huntington Beach in Southern California caused more than 100,000 gallons (378,541 L) of oil to spill into the ocean. The spill contaminated ocean waters and beaches and killed wildlife. For instance, the oil spread throughout a coastal preserve called the Talbert Wetlands. "The oil has infiltrated the entirety of the (Talbert) Wetlands. There's significant impacts to wildlife there," said Orange County supervisor Katrina Foley. "These are wetlands that we've been working with the Army Corps of Engineers, with the Land Trust, with all the community wildlife partners to make sure to create this beautiful, natural habitat for decades. And now in just a day, it's completely destroyed."[39]

The world's oceans have struggled with the constant barrage of pollutants resulting from human activity. It is not just those who live close to the oceans that are causing that pollution. As the Natural Resources Defense Council explains, everyone shares responsibility for ocean pollution. The organization says, "By their very nature—with all streams flowing to rivers, all rivers leading to the sea—the oceans are the end point for so much of the pollution we produce on land, however far from the coasts we may be."[40]

CHAPTER FOUR

Overuse

Sharks are thought to have existed for hundreds of millions of years, and they have always played an important role in keeping the oceans healthy by helping maintain balance and diversity of species. However, these ancient creatures are in danger. Every year, people kill millions of sharks, both intentionally and unintentionally, and as a result the number of sharks in the oceans is steadily declining. According to a 2021 article in *Nature*, the global population of sharks decreased 71 percent from 1970 to 2018. The authors state, "In total, half (16 out of 31) of oceanic shark species are now critically endangered . . . or endangered."[41]

People kill sharks for their meat, organs, fins, and skin, which are used for food, medicine, and other products. When they kill too many, as has been happening with sharks and many other ocean creatures, marine ecosystems suffer. The delicate balance that keeps oceans healthy is threatened by overuse.

Unsustainable Fishing

One of the biggest overuse problems is unsustainable fishing. People eat a wide variety of seafood, and they are harvesting more and more of it from the oceans every year. According to a 2020 report by the Food and Agriculture Organization of the United Nations (FAO), world fish consumption increased about 3 percent every year from 1961 to 2017. In 2018 the European Commission estimated that worldwide, the average person eats almost 50 pounds (22.7 kg) of seafood per year. It says that China consumes the most overall, followed by the European Union, Japan, Indonesia, and the United States. In addition to ever-increasing demand, another reason that more and more seafood is being harvested is that people have learned how to catch it more easily. Seafood Watch, a program of the Monterey Bay Aquarium, explains, "Technology has revolutionized modern fishing practices. Today, many boats have large trawling gear, satellite navigation, refrigeration and processing equipment on deck. This makes it possible to find fish more efficiently, catch lots of fish quickly and stay at sea longer."[42] The organization explains that all of these advances have made it possible for people to catch more fish than is healthy for the diversity of sealife in the oceans.

Overuse is bad for ocean ecosystems because it means that the sealife will not be able to replenish what has been taken. For instance, if fewer sharks are taken out of the oceans, there will be enough left to reproduce and replace those that were killed. This is known as sustainable fishing. If too many sharks are killed, however, the remaining shark population will not be large enough to replace what has been taken. This is unsustainable fishing. In much of the world, people are now fishing unsustainably. As a result, populations of fish and many other marine creatures are de-

Shark meat is a popular food around the world, and manufacturers also use shark cartilage in some medicines. These uses and a general fear of these predators lead to the widespread killing of sharks.

Hunting Whales to the Point of Extinction

Humans have a long history of hunting whales. They have hunted them for their oil, their meat, and other parts of their bodies. By the twentieth century they had nearly hunted them out of existence. According to the Environmental Investigation Agency, "In the 20th century alone, an estimated 2.9 million great whales were killed by the commercial whaling industry, thought to be the largest destruction of biomass in human history, with some species including the blue whale reduced in population size by up to 90%."

Whales play an important part in keeping the oceans healthy—for example, helping various nutrients cycle through the ecosystem. Their loss thus harms the overall health of the oceans.

In order to prevent the complete extinction of whales, many countries finally began passing laws banning or limiting whaling. The United States banned whaling in 1971, and in 1982 the International Whaling Commission passed a worldwide moratorium on commercial whaling. This has allowed whale populations to increase. Not all countries abide by the moratorium. Japan, Iceland, and Norway continue to hunt whales, although they impose limits on the number that can be killed.

Environmental Investigation Agency, "The State of the Ocean," 2021. https://eia-international.org.

clining, with some in danger of extinction. Greenpeace says that many types of fish are being fished unsustainably: "We've already removed at least two-thirds of the large fish in the ocean, and one in three fish populations have collapsed since 1950. Put simply, there are too many boats chasing too few fish."[43] The FAO agrees. This organization monitors fish resources. It finds that in 1974, 90 percent of fish stocks were at biologically sustainable levels, meaning that there were enough of them to ensure that the population could continue to replenish itself into

> "We've already removed at least two-thirds of the large fish in the ocean, and one in three fish populations have collapsed since 1950."[43]
>
> —Greenpeace, an organization that works to defend the natural world

the future. However, by 2017 (the most recent estimate available) the FAO reported that only about 69 percent of fish stocks were biologically sustainable.

Waste in Fishing

Even worse, a significant percentage of the marine creatures killed by fishers do not even end up feeding people. Instead, many are simply wasted. Some waste happens when a catch spoils during transportation, or later when consumers do not eat it before it goes bad. However, a lot of the waste occurs when fish and other creatures are thrown back into the ocean because they were not the desired catch. For instance, a commercial fishing boat that goes out for tuna or halibut will likely also catch other types of fish or sea creatures in its nets or lines. Because of the types of nets and lines commonly used in commercial fishing, it is almost impossible not to do that. These accidental catches are referred to as bycatch, and they are usually thrown back into the ocean. In most cases, though, bycatch does not just go back to living in the ocean; instead, it is often injured or killed in the process of being accidently caught. Overall, a lot of waste occurs in fishing. The FAO estimates that every year, more than a third of the global harvest from fisheries is lost or wasted.

Some commercial fishing practices also snare whales and dolphins. Researchers believe that hundreds of thousands of these creatures die this way every year. Whales and dolphins breathe air like people do, so if they get caught in a net and cannot get to the surface to breathe, they die. The organization Whale and Dolphin Conservation talks about whales in particular, explaining that even when these mammals escape entanglement, an encounter with a fishing boat can still cause injury or death. Fishing lines or other gear sometimes wraps around a whale's head, tail, flippers, or body—causing physical injury or harming the animal's ability to swim or eat. "Entangling gear can make it more difficult for whales to feed, and sometimes the gear cuts into their flesh and bones, leaving the whale to die from resulting infections or starvation,"[44]

Sea Turtles in Danger

Of all the ocean creatures being threatened by human activity, sea turtles are one of the species that is experiencing the greatest harm. Pollution and climate change are both threats to sea turtles. However, the World Wildlife Fund argues that the biggest problem for turtles is the fishing industry. The organization explains, "The single greatest threat to most sea turtles is fishing gear. Hundreds of thousands of turtles are accidentally caught by gillnets, shrimp trawl nets and on longline hooks each year." Sea turtles are extremely important to ocean ecosystems. For example, they help keep the populations of plants and creatures that they eat in check, and they also become food for a number of other animals. Scientists worry that if there are no turtles, there could be negative impacts on many other ocean plants and animals. The nonprofit organization See Turtles explains, "Healthy oceans need sea turtles. Sea turtles are a 'keystone species,' which means they are an important part of their environment and influence other species around them. If a keystone species is removed from a habitat, the natural order can be disrupted, which impacts other wildlife and fauna in different ways."

World Wildlife Fund, "Protecting Turtles from the Threat of Bycatch," 2021. www.worldwildlife.org.

See Turtles, "Why Are Sea Turtles Important?" www.seeturtles.org.

explains Whale and Dolphin Conservation. Because whales live together in groups, with every individual playing an important role, injury or death to one member of the group can threaten the survival and culture of the entire group.

Destructive Fishing Practices

Marine creatures are also threatened by fishing practices that destroy ocean habitat. Bottom trawling is one common type of destructive fishing practice. In bottom trawling, weighted nets are dragged along the floor of the ocean to catch shrimp, crabs, flounder, and other seafloor-dwelling species. The Marine Conservation

Institute explains just how destructive this is. It says, "A large net with heavy weights is dragged across the sea-floor, scooping up everything in its path. These nets are capable of destroying enormous swaths of fragile seafloor habitats, including fragile cold-water coral and sponge ecosystems. Once destroyed, these ancient and ecologi-cally vital communities may take de-cades or longer to recover."[45]

Bren Smith has worked as a commercial fisher. He talks about the damage caused by bottom trawling, saying, "We ripped up entire ecosystems with our trawls. After each haul, we threw dead bycatch—basically, anything that comes up other than what you're fishing for—overboard by the thousands; our ship was sur-rounded by a sea of death."[46]

Another type of destructive fishing practice is blast fishing, in which dynamite or other types of explosives are thrown into the water. The resulting explosions create shock waves that stun or kill fish. These fish can then be easily collected and brought aboard the boat. But in the process, the explosions often de-stroy coral reefs and kill or injure large numbers of sea creatures. Typically, those dead or dying creatures are just left behind. Al-though blast fishing is illegal in most countries, it is still done because it can result in a very large catch. Ocean conservation organization ReefCause says, "Whereas as a net fisherman can catch about six pounds of fish on a good day, blast fishing can yield about 20 pounds on a normal day and up to 45 pounds on a good day."[47] The organization explains that while blast fishing harms ecosystems and reduces the amount of fish in the long term, it continues to happen because for many in this business, simply feeding their families is more important that looking after the environment.

This bottlenose dolphin has drowned after becoming entangled in a commercial fishing net in the Mediterranean Sea. Hundreds of thousands of whales and dolphins meet this fate each year.

Illegal Fishing Practices Are Difficult to Stop

While many destructive fishing practices are illegal, that does not stop them from happening. Overall, illegal fishing practices are widespread and have proved difficult to eliminate. Many experts report that it is relatively easy to use illegal practices because there is not a strong system of enforcement in most places. Further, once illegally caught seafood becomes mixed with what has been legally caught, it is impossible to know the difference between the two. Seafood Watch characterizes illegal fishing practices as a global problem when it says, "Illegal, unreported and unregulated fishing—or IUU fishing—accounts for one of every five wild-caught fish. Some experts estimate that 10–26 million tons of IUU-caught fish is taken each year—an amount equal to 11–19 percent of the global reported catch."[48]

Many of those who work in commercial fishing understand why certain practices are illegal and abide by those rules. They realize that overuse, waste, or destruction of valuable ocean resources can decimate fish populations and ultimately destroy their own livelihoods. However, those who choose to ignore the rules find many ways to avoid detection. They might transfer their catch from one ship to another or fly the flag of another country in order to confuse authorities. They might dock in ports that are known to lack inspectors or where inspectors accept bribes.

A bottom trawler works off the coast of Biloxi, Mississippi. These boats carry huge nets that scrape across the sea floor, scooping up everything in their path.

Sometimes people who are trying to fish illegally even disable identification and monitoring systems. Large fishing boats are commonly required to use transponders that show their location. Bjorn Bergman is a data analyst at a nonprofit organization called Global Fishing Watch, which uses satellites to track ships at sea, looking for those that have purposely turned off these transponders in order to hide illegal activity. When Bergman notices suspicious activity, he notifies authorities so that they can take a closer look, and in some cases this has led to catching illegal fishing. For example, in 2016 he was looking at transponder signals from six Chinese ships in the southern Indian Ocean and noticed some unusual signal patterns. He notified the authorities, who sent patrols to investigate. Journalist Olive Heffernan explains what they found: "The entire fleet was using banned drift nets laid out over kilometres of ocean, ensnaring species such as tuna, sharks, turtles and dolphins. The trawlers were attaching . . . [beacons with transponders] to the nets so as not to lose them, which explained the pattern Bergman had noticed."[48] The fleet was eventually stopped, and the owner was fined almost $1 million. However, experts widely agree that illegal fishing such as this is very common and that many illegal practices go uncaught and unpunished.

The oceans are one of humankind's most valuable resources. For a long time, people have taken whatever they wanted from those oceans. However, there is a growing realization worldwide that this is causing harm and that if the world looks after the oceans instead, they will continue to be a valuable resource. As the Organisation for Economic Co-operation and Development explains, "If managed sustainably, the ocean has the capacity to regenerate, be more productive, [and] resilient."[50]

CHAPTER FIVE

Keeping the Oceans Healthy

There is widespread evidence that the world's oceans are in trouble. However, there is also evidence that the oceans have a remarkable ability to heal. A team of marine ecologists recently took a closer look at the health of some key habitats and species in the oceans, assessing the results of various marine restoration efforts. They found that many conservation efforts have led to substantial improvements in habitats and species numbers. Their conclusion: despite the many harms that have been inflicted on the oceans, recovery is possible—but only if the world acts quickly and boldly to protect them. Says researcher Carlos M. Duarte, "We concluded that it is possible to achieve a substantial rebuilding of marine life, to between seventy per cent and ninety per cent of its past wealth by 2050."[51] However, Duarte adds, achieving that goal will not happen without significant change.

Reducing Emissions

Many nations have recognized that climate change is a serious threat to the oceans and the planet in general and that society needs to take action to mitigate that change by reducing harmful emissions. Some countries have made substantial progress in limiting emissions. For example, Morocco has reduced emissions by greatly increasing the use of renewable energy such as solar and wind power. Journalist Aida Alami explains, "Morocco has made a name for itself as a climate leader. Renewables make up almost two-fifths of its electricity capacity, some fossil fuel subsidies have been phased out and the country lays claim to some of the world's largest clean energy projects. The country has received much praise for its actions to decarbonise."[52]

However, most countries have not been so successful. Overall, the world is simply not reducing emissions enough to prevent great future harm to the oceans. Under the Paris Agreement on climate change, which was adopted in 2015, approximately 190 countries have committed to the goal of reducing global greenhouse gas emissions to limit the global temperature increase in this century to 2°C.

These countries have submitted detailed plans, called nationally determined contributions (NDCs), to show how they will accomplish this goal. It is widely believed that warming greater than that will be very harmful to the oceans and to life all over the earth. Yet assessments on progress made toward that goal show that most countries are falling far short. In 2021 the United Nations

Wind farms, like this one in Morocco, can produce renewable energy to reduce the emissions associated with carbon-based fuels.

made an assessment of existing NDCs and progress toward the Paris Agreement. That assessment resulted in what the United Nations described as "some worrying findings." Rather than seeing the hoped-for decrease in greenhouse gas emissions, the assessment revealed that a 16 percent increase is likely to occur worldwide between 2010 and 2030. The United Nations warned, "Such an increase, unless actions are taken immediately, may lead to a temperature rise of about 2.7C by the end of the century."[53]

Ko Barrett, vice chair of the Intergovernmental Panel on Climate Change, stresses that nations around the world need to do a lot more than they are doing if they want to prevent environmental disaster. "It is still possible to forestall most of the most dire impacts, but it really requires unprecedented, transformational change,"[54] says Barrett. Most experts agree that such transformational change is not happening so far.

Decreasing Plastic Pollution

Reversing other threats to ocean health has proved almost as difficult as reducing greenhouse gases. When it comes to all the plastic in the oceans, it seems that much of what is already there may be there to stay. Most experts agree that it would be extremely difficult to clean up all the plastic that has already accumulated. The Sea Education Association explains, "Because most of the plastic in the ocean is in very small fragments there is no practical way to clean it up. One would have to filter enormous amounts of water to collect a relatively small mass of plastic—in a typical net tow that filters about 120,000 gallons of water, the plastic pieces collected would fit in the palm of your hand." Additionally, the organization explains that nets that catch plastic would also catch small beneficial organisms like plankton. It says, "This could end up causing more harm than good."[55]

"Because most of the plastic in the ocean is in very small fragments there is no practical way to clean it up."[55]

—Sea Education Association, a nonprofit educational organization

Restorative Farming

Bren Smith is a restorative ocean farmer. He grows crops that can be used as food or fuel for people and also help restore marine environments as they are farmed. This method of farming is thought to be one way of restoring ocean health. Smith grows shellfish and seaweed. He describes what he does: "Picture my farm as a vertical underwater garden: hurricane-proof anchors on the edges connected by horizontal ropes floating six feet below the surface. From these lines, kelp and other kinds of seaweed grow vertically downward, next to scallops in hanging nets . . . and mussels held in suspension in mesh socks. On the seafloor below sit oysters in cages."

Smith explains that his farming is good for the environment because oysters and mussels filter the seawater, and seaweed absorbs large amounts of carbon. Not only do these creatures improve the environment, they can be used for food and do not require any fertilizer or any other input. "They simply grow by soaking up ocean nutrients, making it, hands down, the most sustainable form of farming on the planet," he says.

Bren Smith, *Eat Like a Fish: My Adventures as a Fisherman Turned Restorative Ocean Farmer*. New York: Knopf, 2019, pp. 9–10.

The best that can be done at this point, many experts believe, is to stop adding more plastic to the oceans. One way to do this is to create new materials that would take the place of traditional plastics. A number of different companies are already creating a more sustainable type of plastic known as bioplastic. Unlike traditional plastics, which are made from petroleum, bioplastic is made from various plant-based materials, such as corn. Because bioplastic production does not rely on petroleum, that process is generally better for the environment. And unlike traditional plastics, bioplastic is usually biodegradable.

Corn is just one plant that can be used to make bioplastic. Hemp is another. The Hemp Foundation explains that hemp-based plastic has many benefits. It says, "In contrast to the conventional plastic, hemp plastic is absolutely chemical-free and not a constant source of pollution to the environment. It can be recycled indefinitely and takes about 3–6 months to decompose. Even if you don't recycle hemp plastics, it is not a threat to nature as it will continue to break down into its basic form in no time and decompose."[56] However, while bioplastic has many benefits, it is still not used in large quantities worldwide because scientists have not yet been able to produce bioplastic that is as strong, versatile, or cheap as traditional plastic.

Environmentalists also stress that while the world needs alternatives to petroleum-based plastic, the solution to plastic pollution must include simply using less of it. Many cities around the world have banned single-use plastic bags. Many restaurants have stopped giving out plastic straws. Many individuals have switched from plastic storage and sandwich bags, which are often tossed out after one use, to reusable containers. Although these are small steps, they contribute to the larger effort to prevent plastic from reaching the world's oceans. The NOAA Marine Debris Program explains, "If you think about an overflowing sink, the first step before cleaning up the water is to turn the tap off. That is exactly how prevention works. By acting to prevent marine debris, we can stop this problem from growing."[57]

Increasing Sustainable Fishing Practices

Just as people need to be careful about what goes into the ocean, they also need to be mindful of what they take out of it. Adoption and enforcement of sustainable fishing practices can go a long way toward protecting ocean health. This means leaving enough fish in the ocean to ensure that populations do not get smaller over time, as well as fishing in a way that does not harm the ocean habitat or any of the other creatures that live in that habitat. Fisher Chris Brown talks about how he learned the importance of sustainable fishing from his grandfather. He says, "Sometimes, we'd haul up the net and it would be full of juvenile fish. My grandfather would look over and say, 'Don't eat your seed corn, boy.' That was him telling me it's not okay to catch juvenile fish. Another saying he had was, 'You can only kill fish once, so make sure that the day you do, you sell them.' The lesson in all of it: Don't waste."[58]

Individuals can support sustainable fishing by trying to only eat seafood that was harvested sustainably. This means doing some research. Seafood Watch explains, "To know if your seafood is from an environmentally responsible source, you have to know what kind of fish it is, where it was harvested and how it was caught or farmed."[59] Some organizations have websites or apps that help consumers do this research. For example, Seafood Watch's website allows people to search different types of fish and the ocean in which it was harvested in order to see whether that fish was likely to have been sustainably caught. For example, a shopper who plans to buy tilapia to cook for dinner, would type "tilapia" into the Seafood Watch Consumer Guide, and see a list of the best choices, good alternatives, and species of

> "To know if your seafood is from an environmentally responsible source, you have to know what kind of fish it is, where it was harvested and how it was caught or farmed."[59]
>
> —Seafood Watch, a group that promotes sustainable fishing

Labels placed on the fish counter in a grocery store identify the seafood as being sustainably sourced. This helps consumers make environmentally responsible choices.

...stainably Sourced
...EAFOOD
...ook for these labels.

 Wild Caught

 Responsibly Farmed

 Wild Caught Alaska

 Responsibly Farmed

tilapia to avoid. The site explains the reason for the particular ratings and provides a description of its criteria.

Consumer demand can bring about change. If consumers start requesting sustainably sourced seafood, sellers and distributors are more likely to supply it. This demand would also encourage the fishing industry to change its practices.

Changes have been taking place. A 2021 Environmental Defense Fund report summarizes worldwide progress toward sustainable fishing. Since the 1990s many countries have implemented sustainable fishing regulations. This has led to noticeable improvements in the state of fish populations, the report notes. In the United States in the 1970s and 1980s, for instance, fishing laws were mostly dictated by economics and politics, with little consideration for ocean health. As the US fishing industry has shifted to sustainable practices, the improvement has been noticeable. The report notes that "47 stocks of fish have been rebuilt after being overfished and only 49 stocks out of 465 remain in an overfished condition."[60]

According to NOAA Fisheries, the United States now scientifically monitors and manages its fisheries in order to ensure sustainability. The agency says:

- By law, U.S. seafood must be caught according to fishery management plans that:
- Consider social and economic outcomes for fishing communities.
- Prevent overfishing.
- Rebuild depleted stocks.
- Minimize bycatch and interactions with protected species.
- Identify and conserve essential fish habitat.[61]

While such progress is good, a lot more needs to be done. This is especially true in less developed countries. In these countries

The Problem with Plastic Recycling

Many people think that recycling is a good way to reduce the problem of plastic accumulating in the oceans. For instance, in 2020 and 2021 the Nippon Foundation surveyed thousands of people around the world. When asked "How is the general public contributing to ensuring ocean sustainability?," the top answer, given by 67 percent of people, was "recycling plastic waste."

However, what many people do not realize is that most plastic is never recycled. Sandra Ann Harris is the founder of ECOLunchbox, a company that sells plastic-free food containers that individuals can use as an alternative to plastic. She says, "Recycling has been heralded for decades as the panacea for plastic dependence, with feel-good products made from recycled plastic like polyester fleece jackets, skateboards, sunglasses, shoes, and toys." Unfortunately, she maintains, "the trouble is that lots of dirty, low quality, or non-conforming plastic, such as items without sorting codes stamped on the bottom, have never been able to be recycled." Overall, says Harris, "only 1–5 percent of global discarded plastics have ever really been recycled."

Quoted in World Ocean Initiative, "New Surveys Reveal Heightened Concern About Ocean Pollution," March 30, 2021. https://ocean.economist.com.

Sandra Ann Harris, *Say Goodbye to Plastic: A Survival Guide for Plastic-Free Living.* Hobart, NY: Hatherleigh, 2020, p. 36.

many people are more focused on feeding their families than following sustainable practices. But many of these practices would benefit them as much as anyone else. Showing them those benefits, and teaching them how to fish sustainably with the tools they already have, could go a long way toward protecting fish populations.

Increasing Marine Protected Areas

Another way to protect the ocean and allow it to recover from the effects of human activity is to create protected areas. Marine protected areas (MPAs) are parts of the ocean where there are limits on what people can do. In some protected areas all human activity is prohibited, while others just have restrictions, such as limits on how many fish can be caught. The Galápagos Islands are a well-known protected area. These islands are home to creatures and plants that are not found anywhere else in the world. Some fishing is allowed in the Galápagos Islands, but it is subject to strict regulations.

Biologists have found that MPAs allow declining populations of plants and animals to recover and become much healthier overall. This is what happened in one MPA in New Zealand. This area, researchers write, "was able to go from a sea urchin barren—an ecosystem destroyed by overgrazing from an unchecked and exploding population of sea urchins—back to its original kelp forest ecosystem within 12 years of its designation. The shelter offered by the fully protected MPA allowed for an increase in the abundance of sea urchin-eating fish, resulting in an overall increase in local biodiversity."[62]

Overall, MPAs still make up only a small percentage of the total area of the oceans. As a result, many people insist that more

A healthy humpback whale breaches in the Southern Ocean. This region, with its huge populations of whales, krill, fish, and other species, is in particular need of protection from environmental harm.

protected areas and more effective protections are needed. The United States has more MPAs than many other nations. According to NOAA, the nation has about one thousand such areas, making up about a quarter of its waters. The Marine Protection Atlas ranks the United States fourth in the world for protections. The island nation of Palau is ranked first. Yet while some parts of the oceans are protected, many more are in need of protection. For instance, the Pew Charitable Trusts has called for the creation of protected areas in the Southern Ocean, which is around Antarctica. It explains:

> This region . . . is home to thousands of species found nowhere else, from colossal squid and fish with antifreeze proteins in their blood, to bioluminescent worms and brilliantly hued starfish. . . . These waters are vital to the health of the planet, producing strong upwelling currents that carry critical nutrients north of the equator and, in concert with the rest of the ocean, play a role in regulating the climate.[63]

The Pew Charitable Trusts wants to create protected areas to shield this part of the ocean from the increasing harm it is experiencing from industrial fishing. Doing so will require international cooperation.

While there are many challenges to protecting the oceans, they do deserve and need protection. These vast bodies of water support and inspire life all over the world. To live without them is both unimaginable and impossible. Tom Dillon, who oversees conservation and environmental initiatives for the Pew Charitable Trusts, writes, "Since the dawn of humankind, the ocean has elicited nearly every imaginable emotion—respect, gratitude, humility, awe, curiosity, fear. And no wonder: The seas feed us, dictate much of our weather, shape our lands, produce half the oxygen we breathe, spawn life-changing storms, and harbor more biodiversity than any ecosystem on land."[64] Quite simply, healthy oceans are essential for life on earth.

SOURCE NOTES

Introduction: More Important than Most People Realize

1. Philip J. Landrigan et al., "Human Health and Ocean Pollution," *Annals of Global Health*, December 3, 2020. https://annalsof globalhealth.org.
2. Karen Sack, "Protecting Ocean Health Will Protect the Health of Humankind," *UN Chronicle*, June 8, 2020. www.un.org.
3. Quoted in Stephen Leahy, "Climate Change Driving Entire Planet to Dangerous 'Tipping Point,'" *National Geographic*, November 30, 2019. www.nationalgeographic.co.uk.
4. Quoted in UN News, "'Simply No Scenario' Where Humanity Can Survive on an Ocean-Free Planet," June 1, 2021. https://news.un.org.

Chapter One: The Importance of the Oceans

5. United Nations Environment Programme, "Why Do Oceans and Seas Matter?" www.unep.org.
6. National Geographic Society, "Ocean," October 21, 2019. www.nationalgeographic.org.
7. United Nations Educational, Scientific and Cultural Organization, "Ocean Life: The Marine Age of Discovery," 2021. https://en.unesco.org.
8. National Ocean Service, "How Much Oxygen Comes from the Ocean?," February 26, 2021. https://oceanservice.noaa.gov.
9. Sean Fleming, "Here Are 5 Reasons Why the Ocean Is So Important," World Economic Forum, August 29, 2019. www.weforum.org.
10. National Oceanic and Atmospheric Administration, "How Does the Ocean Affect Climate and Weather on Land?" https://ocean explorer.noaa.gov.
11. Fleming, "Here Are 5 Reasons Why the Ocean Is So Important."
12. Quoted in Craig Welch, "Sea Change: Food for Millions," *Seattle Times*, December 21, 2013. http://apps.seattletimes.com.
13. Quoted in Marla Cimini, "'Blue Mind': Why Being Near the Water Makes You Happy," *USA Today*, November 13, 2017. www.usatoday.com.

14. Marine Conservation Institute, "Why Protect the Ocean?," 2020. https://marine-conservation.org.

Chapter Two: Climate Change

15. Ocean Conservancy, "Heatwave in the Pacific Northwest," August 4, 2021. https://oceanconservancy.org.
16. World Weather Attribution, "Western North American Extreme Heat Virtually Impossible Without Human-Caused Climate Change," July 7, 2021. www.worldweatherattribution.org.
17. Hans-Otto Pörtner et al., "Summary for Policymakers," International Panel on Climate Change, 2019. www.ipcc.ch.
18. Nick Bond, "So What Are Marine Heatwaves?," NOAA Research, October 8, 2019. https://research.noaa.gov.
19. Lucy Sherriff, "The Scientists Fighting to Save the Ocean's Most Important Carbon Capture System," *Washington Post*, July 5, 2021. www.washingtonpost.com.
20. National Science Foundation, "Collapse of Northern California Kelp Forests Will Be Hard to Reverse," March 17, 2021. www.nsf.gov.
21. Lauren Sommer, "Fearing Their Kids Will Inherit Dead Coral Reefs, Scientists Are Urging Bold Action," *Morning Edition*, NPR, May 27, 2021. www.npr.org.
22. Peter Thomson, "State of the Ocean Will 'Ultimately Determine the Survival of Our Species': UN Special Envoy," UN News, January 8, 2021. https://news.un.org.
23. Sarah Kaplan, "A Critical Ocean System May Be Heading for Collapse Due to Climate Change, Study Finds," *Washington Post*, August 5, 2021. www.washingtonpost.com.
24. National Ocean Service, "What Percentage of the American Population Lives Near the Coast?," February 26, 2021. https://oceanservice.noaa.gov.
25. US Environmental Protection Agency, "Climate Change Indicators: Oceans," May 12, 2021. www.epa.gov.

Chapter Three: Pollution

26. National Geographic Society, "Great Pacific Garbage Patch," July 5, 2019. www.nationalgeographic.org.
27. Landrigan et al., "Human Health and Ocean Pollution."
28. Marcus Eriksen, *Junk Raft: An Ocean Voyage and a Rising Tide of Activism to Fight Plastic Pollution*. Boston: Beacon, 2017, pp. 16–17.
29. Will McCallum, *How to Give Up Plastic: A Guide to Changing the World, One Plastic Bottle at a Time*. London: Penguin, 2018, p. 81.
30. Environmental Investigation Agency, "The State of the Ocean," 2021. https://eia-international.org.

31. Quoted in Victoria Gill, "Marine Plastic: Hundreds of Fragments in Dead Seabirds," BBC, June 23, 2018. www.bbc.com.
32. Christina Castillo, "Marine Plastics," Smithsonian Institution Ocean Portal, 2018. https://ocean.si.edu.
33. Oceana, "Oceana Finds Plastic Entangling, Choking 1,800 Marine Animals in U.S. Waters," November 19, 2020. https://usa.oceana .org.
34. US Environmental Protection Agency, "Soak Up the Rain: What's the Problem?," July 12, 2021. www.epa.gov.
35. Josie Fischels, "At Least 600 Tons of Dead Fish Have Washed Up Along Tampa Bay's Shore," NPR, July 13, 2021. www.npr.org.
36. Quoted in Fischels, "At Least 600 Tons of Dead Fish Have Washed Up Along Tampa Bay's Shore."
37. United Nations, "World Oceans Day June 8: Why Ocean Matters." www.un.org.
38. National Oceanic and Atmospheric Administration, "Oil Spills," August 1, 2020. www.noaa.gov.
39. Quoted in Alta Spells et al., "An Oil Spill Off the California Coast Destroyed a Wildlife Habitat and Caused Dead Birds and Fish to Wash Up on Huntington Beach, Officials Say," CNN, October 4, 2021. www.cnn.com.
40. Natural Resources Defense Council, "Ocean Pollution: The Dirty Facts," January 22, 2018. www.nrdc.org.

Chapter Four: Overuse

41. Nathan Pacoureau et al., "Half a Century of Global Decline in Oceanic Sharks and Rays," *Nature*, January 27, 2021. www.nature.com.
42. Seafood Watch, "Avoid Overfishing." www.seafoodwatch.org.
43. Greenpeace, "Oceans Issues and Threats." www.greenpeace.org.
44. Whale and Dolphin Conservation, "Prevent Bycatch." https://us .whales.org.
45. Marine Conservation Institute, "Help Us End Destructive Fishing," 2020. https://marine-conservation.org.
46. Bren Smith, *Eat Like a Fish: My Adventures as a Fisherman Turned Restorative Ocean Farmer*. New York: Knopf, 2019, p. 49.
47. *Conservation* (blog), ReefCause, "The Harmful Effects of Dynamite Fishing on Coral Reefs," April 11, 2021. https://conservation.reef cause.com.
48. Seafood Watch, "Avoid Overfishing."
49. Olive Heffernan, "The Hidden Fight to Stop Illegal Fishing from Destroying Our Oceans," *Wired*, March 3, 2019. www.wired.co.uk.

50. Organisation for Economic Co-Operation and Development, "Sustainable Ocean for All: Harnessing the Benefits of Sustainable Ocean Economies for Developing Countries," 2020. www.oecd.org.

Chapter Five: Keeping the Oceans Healthy

51. Carlos M. Duarte, "Rebuilding Marine Life," *UNESCO Courier*, 2021. https://en.unesco.org.
52. Aida Alami, "How Morocco Went Big on Solar Energy," BBC, November 18, 2021. www.bbc.com.
53. United Nations, "Full NDC Synthesis Report: Some Progress, but Still a Big Concern," September 17, 2021. https://unfccc.int.
54. Quoted in Rebecca Hersher, "A Major Report Warns Climate Change Is Accelerating and Humans Must Cut Emissions Now," NPR, August 9, 2021. www.npr.org.
55. Sea Education Association, "FAQ: Plastic Debris in the Ocean," 2012. www.sea.edu.
56. Vishal Vivek, "How Hemp Can Save the Sea Animals from Extinction," Hemp Foundation, 2019. https://hempfoundation.net.
57. NOAA Marine Debris Program, "Garbage Patches," October 12, 2021. https://marinedebris.noaa.gov.
58. Chris Brown, "Toward Sustainable Seafood: A Fisherman's Story," Walton Family Foundation, March 28, 2017. www.waltonfamily foundation.org.
59. Seafood Watch, "Improve Traceability." www.seafoodwatch.org.
60. Doug Rader, "The Silver Anniversary of Sustainable Fisheries," *EDFish* (blog), Environmental Defense Fund, September 21, 2021. http://blogs.edf.org.
61. NOAA Fisheries, "Understanding Sustainable Seafood." www.fish eries.noaa.gov.
62. Margaret Cooney et al., "How Marine Protected Areas Help Fisheries and Ocean Ecosystems," Center for American Progress, June 3, 2019. www.americanprogress.org.
63. Pew Charitable Trusts, "The Need for a Network of Marine Protected Areas in the Southern Ocean," October 7, 2020. www.pewtrusts.org.
64. Tom Dillon, "Can We Protect the Ocean by 2030?," Pew Charitable Trusts, September 9, 2021. www.pewtrusts.org.

ORGANIZATIONS AND WEBSITES

National Oceanic and Atmospheric Administration (NOAA)
www.noaa.gov
This government agency works to gather information about the natural world—including the oceans—and help people better understand it. The NOAA website includes a wide variety of information on the oceans, fisheries, climate, and weather.

Natural Resources Defense Council (NRDC)
www.nrdc.org
The NRDC believes that people have the right to clean air, clean water, and healthy communities, and it works to protect those rights. Its website contains numerous articles about the ocean.

Ocean Conservancy
https://oceanconservancy.org
The Ocean Conservancy is an organization that works to protect the ocean and educate the public. Its website has information about conservation efforts and the many different threats to ocean health.

Seafood Watch
www.seafoodwatch.org
Seafood Watch works with businesses, governments, and consumers in an effort to increase sustainable fishing. Its website contains articles about sustainability and guides on how to eat sustainably.

US Environmental Protection Agency (EPA)
www.epa.gov
The EPA is a US government agency that works to protect the environment, including coastal areas and oceans. Its website contains information about the oceans and about climate change.

FOR FURTHER RESEARCH

Books

Albert Bates, *Dark Side of the Ocean: The Destruction of Our Seas, Why It Matters, and What We Can Do About It.* Summertown, TN: GroundSwell, 2020.

Alex Rogers, *The Deep: The Secret Life of Our Oceans.* New South Wales, Australia: Wildfire, 2019.

Hannah Testa, *Taking on the Plastics Crisis*. New York: Penguin Workshop, 2020.

Deborah Rowan Wright, *Future Sea: How to Rescue and Protect the World's Oceans*. Chicago: University of Chicago Press, 2020.

Internet Sources

Global Coral Reef Monitoring Network, "Status of Coral Reefs of the World: 2020," 2020. https://gcrmn.net.

Brian Palmer, "High Seas: Few Rules, Fewer Sheriffs," Natural Resources Defense Council, January 16, 2019. www.nrdc.org.

Hans-Otto Pörtner et al., "IPCC Special Report on the Ocean and Cryosphere in a Changing Climate," Intergovernmental Panel on Climate Change, 2019. www.ipcc.ch.

Todd Woody, "California's Kelp Forests Are Disappearing in a Warming World. Can They Be Saved?," *National Geographic*, April 30, 2020. www.nationalgeographic.com.

INDEX

63